Contents

RaW Voices

True Stories of Hardship and Hope

Edited by Vanessa Feltz

Published in 2008 by BBC Books, an imprint of Ebury Publishing,
Ebury Publishing is a division of the Random House Group Ltd.

The Random House Group Ltd Reg. No 954009.
Addresses for companies within the Random House Group can be
found at www.randomhouse.co.uk

A CIP catalogue record for this book is available from the
British Library.

ISBN 9781846074462

The Random House Group Limited supports The Forest Stewardship
Council (FSC), the leading international forest certification
organisation. All our titles that are printed on Greenpeace approved
FSC certified paper carry the FSC logo. Our paper procurement policy
can be found at: www.rbooks.co.uk/environment

Commissioning Editor: Lorna Russell

Cover design by Two Associates
Typeset in Stone Serif by SX Composing DTP, Rayleigh, Essex
Printed and bound in Great Britain by
Cox and Wyman Ltd, Reading, Berkshire

Introduction

I was brought up with books and first learnt to read when I was two. In case I sound like a child genius, let me explain! I used to cross out any word I couldn't read. I remember a book about a pigeon where I crossed out the word 'preposterous'.

We had a book room in our house and it was good to be able to walk in and dip in and out of many different books. My love of books stayed with me and I went on to study English Literature at Cambridge University.

What drew me to RaW Voices was the magic of people discovering the written word. Through my work on TV and radio and as a writer I see many sides of human life. How people cope with huge problems always amazes me. I am often struck by how well or badly human beings treat each other. In this book we see some of that, but we also see how people can find a new world through the power of words.

The stories in *RaW Voices* made me realise that our lives are so full. To be able to find out what other people think and feel is an important part of life. We need the gifts of reading and writing, not just to cope with things like looking up an address, but so we can enjoy books, jokes and perhaps poems. The people you will meet on these pages have taken steps to enrich their lives – one of them not until she was in her seventies.

Stories of real lives are always interesting, because they are a window into another world. Sometimes they are so different from our own lives that we cannot find any links at all. But often a phrase or event really strikes us, and we think, 'I know how that feels!' This is often what makes stories really come to life.

As I read these stories I kept thinking: 'It really is never too late to change your life.' I hope that you enjoy reading them as much as I did.

Vanessa Feltz

The Teacher

If anyone has been dealt a rotten hand in life, Paul Lloyd is that person. He experienced the kind of troubled background that sends you towards prison fast. He shows us what it is like to survive adult life without basic literacy. How do you turn yourself around from having no job, regular stints in prison and no obvious future?

Paul Lloyd

One of my strongest memories of my school days is sitting in the corner of the classroom with the dunce's hat on. The classroom was small, the desks were scarred and the teachers did their best, but they didn't really care. If you were awkward like me, not wanting to learn, answering back, generally being either cheeky or silent, they controlled you with discipline – not the strap, just total humiliation like the dunce's cap. Sitting there, with that hat on, made me feel one of two things. Either I felt utterly useless, despondent and wondered what life was about, or I felt really angry. I wanted to get my own back on these people who thought they were clever and I was stupid. I was nine years old.

I missed a lot of school because I was very ill with polio. Polio is a horrible disease; it makes you different from other people as it affects your leg muscles. In my day it seemed to happen to kids. When I wanted to be out, playing with my mates, it wasn't possible – you can't run properly, kick a ball or even climb the stairs easily. But of course there's a vaccine now, which is great.

When I recovered, I had to wear a brace on my leg, and this singled me out as being different at school. As anyone who's got something a bit unusual about them will tell you, you end up feeling a bit like an animal in the zoo, because people stare at you all the time. If I was called peg-leg once, I was called it a hundred times. I was just never able to catch up on all of the school work I'd missed. There was too much of it, and no one bothered to help me. That wasn't how it was then. My parents didn't try to help either – I think they were struggling enough to cope with my illness.

Looking back, I can see now that I had serious learning difficulties. I am in my fifties, and things like dyslexia didn't really exist when I was young. I was just made to feel stupid. Of course dyslexia existed really, it's just that it didn't have a name. Stupid is a much easier label to give someone, and when they gave it to me it stuck. I thought I was stupid, and so did everyone else. And to be honest, with some of the things I did, maybe stupid was the right word.

I was frustrated and angry so much of the time, and my anger and frustration came out in all sorts of bad behaviour. When children don't get the help they need, they often don't have any other way to ask for that help. They just lash out when they can't express themselves. I became really difficult at home. I wouldn't turn up for meals, fought with my parents, stayed out with my friends.

I got so bad that I was sent to a children's home. There I learned the 'tricks of the trade'. I found out how to hot-wire cars, shoplift and generally be a bad lot. I stole cars and was in trouble with the police throughout my teenage years. No one seemed to care what I did, so I thought why should I care about myself? The only times I felt good were when I was driving a stolen car too fast, or when I managed to crash it so it was a write-off, while I walked away unharmed. Then I could boast to my friends and feel like I was something special. I left school with no qualifications; with nothing at all.

I was in and out of prison many times. The judges all knew me. So did the duty solicitors. The first time I went to prison, I admit I was a bit scared. It did make me wonder what I was doing with my life. But then I got into the routine and in a strange way it made me feel safe. Regular food, regular hours, people who understood me and my life. Everyone knows that prisons are horrible places and yet, while I knew it was the wrong place to be, I sort of fitted in.

The last time I went to prison was when I was 26. It was just the usual – stealing and being caught. Anyway, this time I was given a job helping in the prison library. I couldn't believe I was back in prison again. I was depressed about how often it was happening. But I was surrounded by all these books and gradually it started to dawn on me that this could be a chance for me. Maybe I could start to improve myself.

So during that stint in prison I started to work on my reading. I knew I wasn't a good reader but I felt I could teach myself to get better. In the library I could pick up any book I liked and go through it at my own pace. It was slow at first, but one of the prison officers was really helpful and encouraging. We had to spend a lot of time alone in our cells, and the prison officer used to bring me books and comics to help pass the time and improve my reading. I'll never forget him.

The first books I remember reading were Westerns by an author called J. T. Edson. He was British but he wrote dozens of books about the Wild West in a way that made you feel he had lived there all his life, instead of in a mining village in Derbyshire. There were some great cowboy heroes in his books, with names like Ole Devil and Dusty Fog. The people in his books were a bit different to the ones that I'd seen in films about the Wild West; they were more interesting, and I began to get involved in their stories. Up until that point the only reading I had ever done was comics or anything with pictures, nothing too hard.

The other author I loved was Wilbur Smith. I'd get lost in his books and could imagine myself in the wild, exotic expanses of Africa – not locked up in a prison cell. People think they know what a prison cell is like, but they don't. Would you really want to live in a bathroom? That's what it's like. It's not a hotel room with en-suite facilities. We didn't even have a loo, just a slop-out bucket, whether I was in solitary (which I was for a while when I tried to run away) or when I shared a cell with three others. It's pretty disgusting and just gets cleared out each morning. Can you imagine if they had to let out a prisoner every time they needed a pee? Believe me, you don't want to spend time in Her Majesty's Ritz accommodation.

What I loved about Wilbur Smith was that the stories were full of adventure and risks and danger. I could really escape in them – the feeling was like driving a stolen car, wondering if I were going to be caught but it was all in my imagination. I couldn't get enough of these books, and they gave me a sense of encouragement because when I'd read one I wanted to read another. I really enjoyed my job in the library and, looking back, this was the first step to moving out of my cycle of going in and out of prison. I wish I'd realized that at the time.

When I came out of prison aged 27, I needed a job. I went to Butlins on Barry Island. It wasn't what I'd planned particularly, but they were good enough to give people a chance when their background was not the best, and, although the pay wasn't brilliant, at least it was work. I was on the maintenance crew. It was at

Butlins that I met my wife. We hit it off immediately. For the first time I knew I had met someone I could really believe in and trust. We both had struggled with life and even had the same problems with reading. I think this was why we understood each other so well. We shared the same difficulties.

My wife's life hadn't been much easier than mine, though she'd never got into trouble like me. She was really lucky though, because she's got parents who love her and have been supportive. I really liked them and couldn't believe it when they said positive things about me and how happy they were that I loved their daughter. It was a bit rocky when I told them about being in prison, but I felt I had to tell them because they'd been so good to me and I didn't want to start off on the wrong foot. When we got married, we couldn't even write a cheque properly, and we had to ask her parents to do it for us. That's how bad it was.

Getting and keeping a job had always been a problem for me, because I couldn't fill in forms and I had a prison record. I used to sell fruit machines all over the country using my dad's driving licence – in fairness to him, although he knew it was wrong, he felt it was one of the few things he could do to help me. But I couldn't map read – it was too hard reading the names of the places. So I had to write out the names of towns and cities I had to get to and then cross off the letters one by one when I arrived to check it was the right place. I held down that job until my next jail term, and no one knew I couldn't read.

I was determined to work, so I also got a job cleaning toilets, serving at the bar, doing odd jobs, being a labourer – in fact I did anything that meant I didn't have to fill in a form. We had two kids, and it was even a problem writing notes for school. Our son really struggled, and every time I rang the school to talk to someone about it, they were great but always ended up saying, 'Mr Lloyd, can you please put all this in writing?' Of course I couldn't. I felt incredibly frustrated and ashamed. My son was so like me. He could hardly read or write but he could draw – we were so proud when we realized he had this wonderful talent.

I found a job as a night-time nursing assistant and used to come home from work and help my son with his school work. I did my best, but, obviously, I was struggling too. Eventually he left school with no qualifications – despite all of our best efforts. But we got on well and decided to start up a small business together cleaning wheelie bins. It really took off, and we were delighted with our success – one of the first for both of us.

We expanded to include other people and that was where our business problems started. When you work for yourself, you'll put in the hours – whatever it takes – to make it work. If you work for a company and are employed, you don't always feel the same. So the people we employed didn't put in the hours and didn't do the job properly. At the same time, our lack of education and business skills meant we didn't do things the best way, either. We went bankrupt and it felt like we were back to square one.

I really hit rock-bottom, and because of this I realized that I needed help with my reading and writing or I was never going to get anywhere. We were back living in Wales by then and – strange though this sounds – I just walked into our local college and asked if there were any courses. The people were so helpful and immediately invited me to a creative-writing course that was running that day.

Our work with the wheelie bins had been pretty boring – just cleaning them out, getting wet and trying not to feel cold. So, to take my mind off it, I created this story in my head about all these different characters based on wheelie bins and gave them names. The story was about the funny things that had happened day to day. I wanted to write it down. There were so many ideas in my mind that I wanted to get on to the page, but I just couldn't quite manage it. My teacher immediately understood my problem and helped. She confirmed that I was dyslexic – which I had never realized. It was the first time I wasn't embarrassed about having a go at something like that, and wasn't worried that I'd make a fool of myself.

Having someone tell me that I did in fact have a specific, recognized problem made a huge difference. I knew then that I wasn't stupid or beyond help. I found there were ways to deal with it. I just had to learn them, and that's what I set out to do. It was so satisfying to be able to get those stories down on paper; they really took shape and I had so many ideas. My books got published through the creative-writing course, and I then went on a computer course and set up a website for my books. Before I started those courses, I could never have imagined that one day I would be a published author, setting up his own website to promote his books. It would have seemed as if I were hearing about a different person.

I didn't make any money but the real achievement was in actually doing it. I got a student of the year award from the National Institute of Adult Continuing Education, and my confidence just soared. While I was still studying, my tutor asked if I had ever considered doing a degree course. That was all the encouragement I needed – I got my HND in multi-media, which led to my degree. I don't want to make it sound as if everything just fell into my lap and it was all so easy. It wasn't easy; it was hard work. But everyone on the course pitched in to support each other. Some were good on computers and others had different skills so we all worked together, helping each other. We did all sorts of things, such as creating voice-recognition software so it was easier to write a letter using the computer.

All of this also gave me confidence to give my son advice and help. I persuaded him to go to art college, and I asked his tutor to give him instructions via a tape recorder. This is a fantastic way to help people with reading problems. He brings the tape recorder home each night and I help him with what he has to do. His drawing is brilliant, but he lacks the ability to express himself in writing. I can see my own problems in my son's experience, and

I want him to see that he can get over them, just like I've done. I never want him to feel that total hopelessness that I felt, or feel the same anger and frustration.

My positive experience through education has made me want to help others, and I have just started a two-year teacher-training course. I want to go back into prisons and teach basic maths and English as I hope it may start others off on a new track. It worked for me, and I want to show other people that it can work for them as well. On my first day of training, I struggled with some of the forms, but I am no longer afraid to ask for help and I say when I can't spell something. I don't suffer in silence any more.

My Wheelie Bin books have been popular in local schools, and I often get invited in to talk about them. I helped at a BBC RaW weekend where I read them to the kids and got them to think up stories of their own, something kids are brilliant at doing because they are just naturally imaginative. But I was really there to talk to their parents and to encourage them to get back into education. They really related to my story, and I could tell them there are lots of grants out there to help. People always worry about money. Most of us have to work for a living, but people don't realize that you can do part-time or evening courses, and there is a lot of financial help out there.

The thing I always say is, you may not be able to cure your problems – like my dyslexia – but you can learn to cope with them and work around them. When I was working as a night nurse I had to write every morning 'nothing special' if it had been a quiet night. They were just two simple words, but I had to learn the letters off by heart before I could fill in the form. No one there ever knew what a struggle it was for me, but I did it.

I have also talked to groups of ex-offenders and encouraged them to improve their reading and writing skills. They took it from me because I was the same as them. I knew what it was like to be in prison. What I began learning in that prison library years ago was the turning-point in my life. I want it to be a turning-point for other people too. I want them to have the new beginning that I have had. It could change their lives the way it changed mine – in the best way possible.

The Fitness Trainer

Five years ago Damion Maston was homeless and a drug addict. Would he ever find a job he loves, a sense of purpose, and relationships he can enjoy without zoning out first through drugs or drink? And, if so, what would bring about such a change? Read on and he'll tell you in his own gutsy words.

Damion Maston

Looking back at the young me, I would describe myself as a real nightmare. I got expelled from school at 14 and ran off to live with some fairground people I knew. It seemed like an exciting life, just like being in a film, on the move, doing anything I wanted to do. As a teenager I thought it was great, but that was when my drinking and my drug habit started. I worked on the fairgrounds and used all the money I earned to pay for drink and drugs. It wasn't heavy stuff in those days – mainly beer and dope.

Working in fairs is great because you travel around, but it's a very close-knit community, and, when you're not from the real 'family', they know you're not going to stay. It's just the romance, or an escape. So you're not fully included. Also, it seems really great on a crowded, sunny summer's night, but on a rainy, cold winter's afternoon it's pretty grim! After a few years, I'd had enough of the fairground life and I was ready to come back home. My mum had other ideas though. Every time I tried to move back home, she kicked me out. She had already coped with me up until 14. Now I was older, she knew things hadn't improved.

I couldn't hold down a job. You get a job, and you're really relieved, because that means regular income to keep your habit going. But then you take too much, get too high or too low and don't turn up to work. And they let it go once or twice, but then they realize you're no good, so you get your cards. And then you're left with no income, but with the same desperate craving for drugs.

I had no home and slept on friends' sofas or in hostels if I could get in to them. I had a couple of relationships but nothing that really lasted, which wasn't surprising given the drugs and my general state. My life was like one long weekend that never ended; I spent a lot of time at pubs and clubs. I had hardly any work so there wasn't really any money coming in. I needed the drugs, and to get the drugs I needed money. I thought crime was the easiest way to get it.

So I started stealing to pay for the drugs and then I started wanting more drugs. The crimes got worse and worse, and when I was 20 I was jailed for armed robbery, a couple of burglaries and a lot of petty thefts. I was sentenced to six years. Going to prison was awful but you learn to cope; you have to or you'll go under. Besides, I soon realized I could still get drugs inside because I knew lots of the other prisoners. They had good links with suppliers on the outside, and there were ways to smuggle the drugs into prison.

But then I was moved to a prison further away. I lost my drug contacts, and it wasn't so easy to get drugs. Despite my unhealthy lifestyle, I've always been quite naturally fit. I was given a job helping out in the gym; I'd always loved sport so I thought, why not? It started off as a way to take my mind off not being able to get the drugs I wanted, but it turned into something much more worthwhile. It was only cleaning at first and general helping-out, but the staff encouraged me to get involved in other things. The prison ran courses that the inmates could take to get better qualifications. So I signed up and ended up with a long list of sports qualifications in weightlifting, football and coaching community sport. I also played rugby with the prison team.

My confidence was sky high. I had discovered something at which I was really good – not just the sports aspect but also the studying. I felt like a different person, like someone who didn't need drugs any more just to make them feel alive or to make them forget about life.

But something just switched off when I came out of prison. I think it took me less than a day to start looking for drugs again. I just took up where I had left off. It was as if my other self – the new, confident one – had been left behind in prison and my sad, bad old self was the one who came out. I just couldn't see at the time that I did have the inner strength still to be a confident person, to stick with the sports and the studying.

I went to London with my girlfriend, and there I started taking heroin and crack cocaine. I see now what a horrendous life it was. Our day-to-day life involved stealing to fund our drug habit. In the middle of all this, we had a baby. For most people this would have been a cause for huge celebration, but it wasn't really for us. We were both so heavily into drugs that it badly affected our baby son. He was born a drug addict.

We ended up in a hostel for the homeless and I was rushed to hospital. My body was covered in sores, caused by the drugs and our unhealthy lifestyle. But it was my lungs that were in really poor shape. I sounded as if I had been running a marathon, despite the fact I was just sitting in a chair. I had no energy and was completely listless. My stomach was in a terrible state because of swallowing drugs, so they couldn't give me drugs to help orally. Because of all the heroin injections, my veins were knackered too. I desperately needed help, but I'd got myself into such a physical state that it was very hard to give me the help I needed. I became so ill that I nearly died.

It was when I came out of hospital, still weak and recovering from pneumonia, that it really hit me, how awful I'd allowed my life to become. My relationship then broke up and I felt like I had nothing. The care worker who was trying to help me just sat me down and gave it to me straight, saying, 'You've not got long left to live.' It really shocked me to be told that the way I had been living my life was slowly but surely killing me. It scared me so much that, for the first time, I asked for help and I really meant it. My care worker said he was going to take a chance on me. I knew this was my final chance – I was going to go through drug rehabilitation.

Sending someone into drug rehabilitation costs a lot of money, so the care worker had to make a judgment that I wouldn't mess up and that the rehab would work for me. It's a bit like gambling: there are no sure-fire guaranteed bets that you can win every time. You just don't know exactly what will happen, but you have to be sure that it's a good bet before you risk losing everything. I was enrolled in the rehab programme and sent to a psychiatric hospital in London for eight weeks and then down to a treatment centre in Sussex. The treatment was starting to show results and, for the final part, I went to Weymouth in Dorset.

It was in Dorset that my life really began to change. Someone from Weymouth College came to the treatment centre to tell us about all the courses they offered. Many of those at the centre were around my age, in their twenties. We all knew that people in our age group were supposed to be the computer-savvy generation. But most of us didn't even know how to turn on a computer, let alone how to use it properly. So

21

I signed up for a Fresh Start course in maths, English and computers. It took me back to my school days. I remember how awful it was at school. I mucked around, was always in trouble and of course never worked. Looking back I realize that it never occurred to me that getting qualifications was important so I didn't try. I wish someone had said, because I can still remember the feeling of achievement when I first started reading and studying in prison. Life suddenly had a purpose and I think it would have really helped if I'd known that at school. When I was finally back-on-track after prison and doing the college courses, I was told I was quite gifted at maths. What a shame I'd not found that out at school.

I now had quite a good collection of grades to show that I could stick with studies and see them through. I had new skills to add to the sports qualifications that I'd got in prison. When the college found out about my sports studies, they weren't bothered about the circumstances that I'd been in when I got them. No one at the college judged me. They were just happy to have someone who was keen and had the knowledge they needed for the job. So they offered me some work in the college gym. It started off as just a few hours a week but built up to 30 hours, which was almost a full-time job.

When one of the sports lecturers went on long-term sick leave, I was asked to stand in. I really wanted to give it a go, but I was shocked at how nervous I was. I'll never forget that sick feeling in the pit of my stomach during my first lecture. But I made myself face up to those nerves and when I did, I knew I'd taken a very big, very important step. I got through that first lecture and the next one and all of the others. It was funny to think of me, standing up there, teaching people and seeing them take note of everything I was saying.

It was at this point that I got nominated for an adult-learning award. This was such great recognition. I was proud of my achievements but, more importantly, I knew it gave me a chance to share my life story and my achievements with others and try to help them and inspire them. Once I was off drugs and no longer had that eating away at my life, studying turned my life around. That college gave me so many wonderful things – including the woman with whom I fell in love. We met at college, and we now live together as a real family, along with her son. My own son, who is now in good health after the terrible start he had because of the drugs, comes to stay with us in the holidays.

I didn't stick with the lecturing, although it was a great experience. My real desire is to go into care work and give back what so many wonderful people gave to me. I do lots of voluntary work for organizations that have helped me, and I'm looking for a job in that area. I keep up my fitness work. I have been running a community football team for a few years now. It's brilliant, and we have gone from just a few young kids having a kick-about to a big squad and the top of the local league. I also play semi-professional rugby which was also something I discovered in prison. I look at myself and think back to five years ago. Back then I was a homeless, hopeless drug addict. It's only five years, not long when you think about it. But it seems like a lifetime. Now I have a full and happy life.

What I've noticed is that many people are scared to go back to learning. I was scared too, but I had reached a point where I had nothing left to lose. I'd gotten so far down, I had so little to look forward to or be happy about. I want people to understand that you're never too old to learn something new. And don't ever let anybody tell you that you are too stupid or too slow to learn something new.

Everybody has some talent – everybody. I knew absolutely nothing about computers, but I can use one now.

I know what it's like to have real problems, not niggling little things but problems that can mean life or death, problems that you think you'll never overcome. But I survived them and other people can too. I found a life for myself that I never, ever thought I could have. I want to share my experience with others. My message is that you can achieve anything you want, if you put in the work, whatever your background. Don't ever let the thought of hard work put you off – the results can be more worthwhile that you could ever imagine.

The Speech Therapist

How did a blind Belfast girl come to be called Bolshie Betty? Betty McAlister is brave and oozes humour, but as her story shows, her natural optimism has often been dented by difficulties and by fate.

Betty McAlister

I have always told myself that I am lucky to be alive. My twin brother and I were born prematurely in 1949. He died at birth and I was almost blind. Doctors did what they could to save my sight. I remember having a number of operations and I could even see some bright colours for a while. But when I was about four my sight went completely. We were living in Belfast at the time and my parents sent me to a residential school for the blind there. It must have been difficult for them, and I'm sure they thought it was for the best. My parents were highly skilled working-class people. My dad was a tool-fitter and my mother had worked at a mill until she married and had a family.

They wanted all of their children to do well.

The residential home for the blind was not a great place to be. The staff were strict. They were known as supervisors, a rather official title, that, in later years, was changed to the more kindly 'house mothers' and 'house fathers'. I've tried hard to forget the shortcomings of the place and the times I was unhappy there. I've just put all of that behind me. I don't dwell on it, as I can't see the point in self-pity; it gets you nowhere. It's enough to say that I went from a loving, warm family home into an institution.

Back then, people with disabilities were called handicapped, and children with disabilities weren't even really expected to go to school. But at my residential school we learnt Braille, which for me, because of my age, wasn't really such a big deal. It was the same as other children learning to read and write with books and pens – that was their way to literacy and Braille was mine. It took me about six months to learn. Doing sums was different: we had a funny peg-board system. I was not so good at that and I remember the teacher getting cross with me. They could be cruel and very intolerant.

Despite the conditions there, I enjoyed learning. I had good friends at the school and we helped each other out. Looking back, the school experience toughened me up. It may not have been that good, but it made me stronger and helped me cope and move on to better things. It taught me that I could achieve things even when the situation was not the best. A few of us even fought to do O levels. I was so proud of my good grades in Spanish.

In 1962 the school moved, and we were able to go home at weekends. That was much better for me as it meant I had some family life. When I left school the only choice I had, if I wanted to stay in Northern Ireland, was to go to a workshop for the blind. So I decided to leave Belfast and head for England, where I got a job at the Royal National Institute for the Blind, the RNIB, in London. It was a very big step. But being away at school and being in a big family had made me look after myself. My mother was not keen for me to stay at home as she had four younger children to look after. I remember my dad was really worried about how I would cope, but I decided I would leave home anyway. I wasn't quite 18. It seems so young now, but I had to tell myself that it was time to make my way in the world.

At the RNIB I helped with proof-reading and translation, and I lived in a hostel for the blind nearby. Getting around was OK because everyone at the hostel helped each other. We had white canes, or sticks as they were called then. We gave each other directions that we knew would be helpful – 'Go right, then straight on for three steps'. We all learnt that way. I got to know people both through work and the hostel, and after a while they started calling me Bolshie Betty! It was because I always spoke my mind. I think being blind made me stick up for myself. I hardly remember not being blind, and that is different for some people. You live in your own world and develop your own methods. I was never afraid to ask for help, and you learn to sense things that others would see. Not just things like traffic, but things about people from their voices and attitudes. I never let it hold me back because it was something with which I had always lived.

I then got a place at a community college and learnt telephone and typing skills. Being blind did not stop me getting ahead, and in fact I don't think it made much difference on that course because of the nature of the work. I worked as a telephonist when there was still the old-fashioned plug-board system. This sounds hard if you're blind, but actually it wasn't that different to learning touch-typing – you just get a sense of where things are. We were all kept very busy. I had a good job at the Royal College of Nursing throughout most of the 1970s. When I was 29, I decided that, if I were not going to get married, I needed to look ahead to a different kind of future and would train in another field. I had already taken five O levels and an A level through the RNIB, and I decided to branch out into speech therapy.

The college where I studied was part of Guy's Hospital in central London. It had taken a few blind students before, so it wasn't a problem for me to be accepted there. I was trained in dealing with people with voice problems like stammering, and I graduated with a diploma three years later. It rather amused me that I was blind, yet teaching people to speak properly.

My life had been changing in other ways too. I'd met a wonderful man, and we got engaged. It was so unexpected. I think that sometimes things do happen when you're not expecting them. I really enjoyed planning our future – suddenly a whole host of unexpected things appeared on the horizon. We talked about having a family and setting up our home. My parents were pleased as well, and we planned a trip over to Belfast. Then, before we could marry, my fiancé died. It was 1984, and I was 35 years old.

For a long time I thought my sadness would overwhelm me. I couldn't eat or sleep; sometimes I felt I couldn't breathe for grief. But work helped. I enjoyed working with people who had learning difficulties, and I was still doing language courses. I even did some training with the Central School of Speech and Drama in London. But the strain of living in London and all that had happened got too much for me. I was missing my family, so I went back to live in Northern Ireland. I wanted to spend time with my nephews and nieces, and be around when they were growing up.

It was much more difficult to get work back home, but I did some speech therapy and telephonist work. Eventually, I got a council flat.

In day-to-day life, it's not easy being blind, and when I moved to the flat I decided to train with a guide dog. I knew this would make it easier for me to get around and be less stressful. The dogs go through very intensive training, after which you train with them. I have had three dogs – one very lively golden retriever and then two Labradors. It's a unique relationship, really, and very much a partnership – having a dog is 60 per cent you and 40 per cent them. They make me feel more safe and secure.

After a while I stopped working because my health wasn't good, but I've never stopped studying. Studying gives me a purpose in life and is rewarding in so many ways. It makes my life interesting. I also travel to see friends and my family, including to America to see my sister who lives in Boston. In the end I think you have to grab life, whatever it brings you. It will always be a challenge.

The Activist Executive

Davy Carlin was a black boy growing up on the Falls Road in Belfast. His outsider's view of the Northern Ireland conflict is compelling. So, too, is the uplifting tale of his life so far.

Davy Carlin

I grew up in Northern Ireland in the 1970s. Our family was poor, black and Catholic. It wasn't a good time to be any one of these things, let alone all three! We lived in the Falls Road, the main road through west Belfast. It became one of the most famous streets in the whole of Northern Ireland, because it was at the heart of what people had started to call the Troubles. It's a funny word to describe what was more like a war than just troubles. Murders, shootings and bombings were a part of everyday life. This was one of the most deprived areas in Western Europe and at the time one of the most famous – for all the wrong reasons.

In a place where most people are white, I was often asked by soldiers and journalists to stand next to the famous Republican political murals on the walls of buildings in the Falls Road so they could take my picture. I suppose they thought it was a good illustration of just how complex the Northern Ireland situation was. I remember the peace line going up, to separate the Catholic Republicans on the Falls and the Protestant Loyalists on the neighbouring Shankill Road, and to stop the two communities from harming each other. It was Belfast's version of the Berlin Wall. The peace line became something of a tourist attraction after the Troubles ended, but when I was a child there was nothing attractive about it. In a few places, it was just a white line, like a road marking, but mostly it was a towering brick, steel and iron wall that stretched for miles. Parts of it had gates that were guarded by the security forces.

When people think of Northern Ireland during that time, they think about the violence. But to me, it was my home. My mum had come back from Ireland to England when she was pregnant with me. She had family all round her in Belfast, and it made a big difference to have that support. I lived with my grandmother for a short while in the Ballymurphy area of west Belfast, a Catholic part of the city. Family ties went very deep and, just in our street, I had relatives in ten different houses along the road. It was a good feeling, that feeling of belonging. It was a very close-knit community and we all looked out for each other. We had to.

I think when you feel exposed and vulnerable, having people around who care about you makes a massive difference. If I'd had a bad day at school or a run-in with the local lads, being able to go back to our street and a safe environment meant a lot. I'm sure that's why Mum came back – for those same reasons of security. When Mum married my stepfather I moved back to live with them. Things were crowded at home. I shared a small bedroom with my four brothers and sisters. The house was old, with an outside toilet. We were always in debt, and there never seemed to be enough of anything to go around. My memories are of being really cramped, cold and hungry.

I had a strict Catholic upbringing and was an altar boy at the local church. I went to St Finian's Catholic primary school on the Falls Road. The school was well known in the area for its high standards and was run by an order of Catholic priests. It was the same school to which the Sinn Fein leader Gerry Adams had gone. It was a good school, but the Troubles made life tough for everybody. At home, because there were so many of us in a small house, there was nowhere to have any peace and quiet even to try to do my homework. I've really asked myself if that's just an excuse, but I don't think so. For example, if I couldn't get a space at our table, then I used to do my homework on the stairs – it was the only place to get any privacy. Eventually, I gave up trying, and it wasn't a real surprise when I failed my eleven plus exam.

I suppose my mum did try to make things better for us all, but somehow things never really worked out. When I was ten we moved to another part of Belfast, because Mum was so sick of seeing British soldiers on the streets all the time. She wanted to be in a better area. But we ended up moving to the neighbourhood where the IRA hunger striker Bobby Sands had lived. This was 1980, and he was in the Maze prison by then, where he died a year later. A lot of people were in mourning for Bobby Sands in our area, and there was a great deal of tension after he died. So, once again, it felt like we were in the thick of the Troubles, no matter how hard we tried to get on with normal life.

There were great teachers at the secondary school to which I went, but I had no real back-up at home. Education was not considered very important in my family. For my mum, what was important was that I knew that I was valued as a person, but she didn't realize that education had a vital role to play in that. I left school with two O levels. I remember thinking at the time that it was a shame, because, in my heart, I knew that I could do better. But I just accepted that I was destined to be a low achiever.

At that time in Northern Ireland, many people felt the Catholics were not treated fairly. I don't know if it was really true, but the accepted view was you got a job depending on your postcode. The province was so divided between Catholic and Protestant that if you just said where you lived, people would usually guess straight away which one you were.

At that time the Protestants had a lot more power and influence than the Catholics, and because my area was strongly Catholic Republican – not Protestant Loyalist – that meant I could only hope to get a menial, low-paid job. The only one I could find was stacking toilet rolls. I did it for three months and was made redundant just before Christmas. I was young, so I just thought it was bad luck and tried to make the best of it, but I'll never forget how awful it was for the married men who worked there. They'd lost their jobs just before Christmas, and they probably had no idea how they were going to support their families without money coming in. How would they put food on the table or give their kids a good Christmas? I watched some of them, grown men, break down in tears.

I decided to look elsewhere in Belfast and moved to the south of the city and here, for the first time in my life, I actually met Protestants and got to know them. Despite all the bad things I had been told and had grown up believing, I realized that Protestants were just ordinary people like me. It was the start of seeing life differently, of realizing that experience could help you think for yourself and make up your own mind about things.

No matter what was going on in my life, the one place to which I had always gone as a kind of escape from everyone and everything was the Whiterock Library in west Belfast. It was like walking into another world, a world where it didn't matter who I was, or what religion I was, or what colour I was or where I lived. I could read whatever I wanted and find out about anything. I wanted to know about that wide world far away from Northern Ireland, about other countries. I read almost every travel book I could find in that library, and I decided that I wanted to see some of those other countries.

I had this goal to travel, but I knew that just wanting something isn't enough – you have to do everything you can to make it happen. I knew I had to work as hard as I possibly could to save money to pay for my travels, so I took on lots of odd jobs. I didn't mind what I did or how much overtime I had to work. I saved every penny until I had enough for my plane ticket and to keep me going. I set off – a Belfast boy leaving behind not just the Troubles, the violence, but also my family and my friends, all the familiar things I had known all my life. But I was ready to go, and travelling all over America, Africa and Europe opened my eyes to how different cultures and people lived together. It was so different from the segregation in Northern Ireland.

When I came back in 1993 the Child Support Agency was opening in Belfast, and they were looking for staff. I applied for a junior job and got it, but I knew I wouldn't be happy just with that. I looked into all of the training courses and used every single opportunity they offered – courses, computer facilities, the lot – as well as still using the local library as a study base. I couldn't afford the internet at home so the library was vital. It also offered all sorts of classes, which were free. I told myself that it was never too late to learn, to study and to teach myself new things. I got more qualifications and was promoted regularly.

It was strange that I had struggled so much at school, but when I returned I felt so much more motivated. To some extent I think that the travel made a big difference in my life. It broadened my horizon, not only because of the different experiences but also because it made me look at my life again. I realized that, deprived as I thought I was, I had opportunities that young men in Africa or South America would never, ever be offered. It made me start to appreciate what was available, and made me determined to make the most of it. I don't think I'd ever felt like that about educational opportunities before.

I also got involved with a trade union, the Northern Ireland Public Service Alliance, or NIPSA, as it was known. What was important for me was that it spoke out for people who felt they did not have a voice and had no power to make themselves heard. It offered them support and opportunities and, most importantly for Northern Ireland at the time, it brought together Protestants and Catholics. I became the chairman of our branch, and we even started our own newspaper. If you'd asked me before I went travelling if I'd be a chairman of something like that, I'd have thought you were mad! Now I wanted to do my best and make the most of the opportunities I had. I didn't really want the responsibility, but I didn't want to shirk it either.

In the mid-1990s some of our staff started getting death threats. As a union we organized a walk-out in protest against the threats. We needed to let the public know what was happening. I spoke at a large rally, something I never thought I could do. I still carried the lack of confidence I'd had since I was a child. You can't shake off those feelings easily. Even though I'd travelled and seen people who must have had much harder lives than me, I knew my experience had been tough too and that lack of encouragement at home has a major effect.

Our public protests helped to focus attention on our situation, and people gave us their full support. I left the union a few years ago to become a manager in a local hospital. For the first time I also had the confidence to take on different voluntary roles in the community. I organized an anti-racist rally that marched along both the Falls Road and the Shankill Road and I became chair of the events committee for the local Make Poverty History group.

I suddenly realized that business and government leaders and others actually respected my work. I had been brought up with the belief that everyone else had more to offer, but by improving my qualifications I gained this new self-confidence. I realized that I also had something to offer. I may not be very academic, but I knew I had something to say.

I am now writing a book, *The Journey*, based on my experiences in Belfast: it's centred on a ride in a black taxi. I am hoping to finish it in the summer of 2008 and then enrol on an Open University course. I haven't decided exactly what I'll study, but it's great to look at all the different courses available and to know that they are open to anyone. I will probably choose social philosophy. I know I'll still have to stay in my job to pay the bills, but that's fine for now.

I am married, and my wife had the same lack of opportunity in her life, but she too is working to change things. I was young when I left school, but my real education has been the one that I've found for myself. Travelling, doing courses, getting training and better qualifications has given me a voice, the confidence to speak out and believe that what I have to say is worth saying; that people want to hear me. I was even interviewed on GMTV about black history in Northern Ireland, and I really enjoyed it.

As a child and a teenager, I saw the television pictures of Northern Ireland, but could I ever have imagined that one day I would be on the television talking about Northern Ireland? I have overcome so many barriers. My philosophy has always been to have a go and try to achieve your dreams. It does not matter if you don't quite make it; at least you have given it your best shot. If you never try, you'll never know.

The Artist

They say every cloud has a silver lining, but, in the case of Ray Jackson, that silver is 100 per cent real. Can a nervous breakdown ever be a blessing? Read Ray's story, and you'll find out that the answer is a resounding 'Yes'.

Ray Jackson

After 30 years of hard work in a good job, I just crumbled. I had a nervous breakdown. I remember the day it happened. I was talking to people at work, but I felt that none of them were listening to me. It was like I was in some sort of film, where I could hear my voice and see everyone getting on with their daily tasks as if I wasn't there. Something inside just exploded and I started to cry. I think the stress of my job had been building up so gradually that I hadn't even noticed it until that moment. I hadn't seen the warning signs. For so long I'd just been focused on earning money and doing well.

I grew up in Wolverhampton. I had left

school with no qualifications or exams at all. None of the teachers seemed worried, and there were no expectations from my parents either, although they encouraged me to get a job. I then trained as a fitter and welder under the City & Guilds. I loved pipe-fitting and knew I was really good at it. It is a craft. I think it appealed to my artistic streak, but I didn't see it that way at the time.

I was also a skilled welder but, with aspirations to get a bigger house and a better life, I knew I needed to earn more money. So I had moved to a better-paid job at a car factory. I doubled my money, which was very important, although it also seemed like I had doubled my hours. I worked my way up from the bottom. As is often the case with promotion, my role got more and more demanding. I worked nights for 25 years. I wasn't very confident, and I found that, as I was promoted, I was spending more and more time trying to pretend that I had better skills than I actually had. Although I was good as a craftsman, the paperwork that goes with it was a nightmare for me. I hated it because I found it so difficult, but I couldn't admit it to anyone. Finally, although I hadn't seen it coming, it simply got too much.

After the breakdown my doctor was really helpful. When I had first seen him a few months before, he had suggested that I might consider changing my job. I thought he'd gone a bit mad and couldn't understand why he wasn't just giving me a prescription rather than trying to change my life. Everyone else, except me, had noticed that I had been under a lot of strain. My wife said that the three months running up to my breakdown had been awful. She had had to be so careful about everything she said or did because I had been so grumpy and snappy all the time.

I had been in this very strange place in my mind, either totally disengaged or focusing on every little detail. It made me highly unpredictable, and no one quite knew what to expect from me – although whatever it was it was manic. The weight of my duties seemed so heavy on my shoulders, and instead of seeing solutions I only ever saw problems. It wasn't just work; it would be little things like whether to drive the car to the shop or walk. It seems silly, but these things take on ridiculous proportions. Everyone else seemed to have a wonderful life with no problems. At work, and sometimes at home, I felt people were selfish and unhelpful, thinking only of themselves, leaving me to sort out all the problems that they created.

I was referred to the local mental health unit, where I had counselling and medical treatment. I also attended their occupational health sessions. For two years I was given good support there. The occupational therapists suggested that I work on my enjoyment of art and my talent for portrait painting. I signed up for a course offered at the hospital that helped people use art as therapy. It was called Art for Health. Breakdowns are awful: you can't face people, family or friends. Going out, ringing people and talking to them are all really difficult, as you just feel totally useless. It's almost like you've forgotten how to function. Anything like art that makes you able to express yourself is really important. Without it you would feel trapped.

I had also always struggled with reading and writing and thought I was dyslexic. So I enrolled in an English course with Wolverhampton Adult Education Service. One of the teachers noticed some of my artwork in one of my books, and he was very impressed by it. I told him that I used to go to painting classes. He thought I had real talent and encouraged me to enrol on a higher education course in art and design. I was really worried and quite nervous about attending the course.

I think this was when I realized the art courses at the hospital had started to make me feel better. I was more in touch with myself. My breakdown meant I'd lost what little confidence I had left and I just didn't know whether I'd be able to handle the course. A side-effect had been that I'd developed a terrible stammer, and I was very self-conscious about that too. But anything seemed better than just being at home, feeling stuck inside four walls and too anxious to venture out; you can start to feel like a prisoner. The first day on this course was a really big thing. I knew I didn't have to go back after the first day if I hated it, but from the very first class I loved it. I couldn't believe I'd actually thought for a moment that I wouldn't do it.

In my old job, people had always called me the 'gadget man'. I could turn my hand to anything, and people often asked me to make things like brackets for hanging baskets or iron wheelbarrows. I'd loved making things, and when I saw that there were sculpture classes on offer, they really appealed to me. I was told that I was gifted in 'three-dimensional disciplines' – which is, I guess, a fancy way of saying I was very good at making things. The course made me realize that I understood and communicated better in artistic ways. It was almost as if I made sense of things through shapes or pictures rather than words. I realized that I could express myself so easily in my art and craftwork, in a way that I found hard to do in reading and writing. This helped to explain the problems I'd had in the past.

I started designing and making silver jewellery. People got to hear about it and orders started to come in. They would describe roughly want they wanted, and I would draw up a design based on that. I'd then go to Birmingham to buy the silver plate and the wire I'd need to make the jewellery. I have lots of happy customers, and my business is now expanding through word of mouth. People also seem to value that handmade quality. They feel they are getting something special and beautiful and unique, not something just knocked out along with a million other identical objects on a factory assembly line.

As my skills grew, my business also grew and I started to feel good about my talent. When that happened, something very strange happened too – I lost my stammer. So in a very real way, I was able to express myself clearly, through not just my work but words as well. One day I went back to visit the mental health unit where I had been treated. I had really liked the occupational therapist who had been my woodwork tutor there, and I wanted to say thank you. One of the women there asked me what I was doing. When they heard about my course, they told me there was a job at the unit, for someone to teach art.

I had already put together a folder with examples of all my art and craftwork, and I felt like a proper artist and craftsman when I brought it back later to show them. They were very impressed and I got the job. At first it was rather like being a supply teacher, just going in whenever I was needed to fill a gap. Then I went in every week, and pretty soon I got a contract.

Working with mental health patients was so rewarding for me. I had been in their situation; I knew what it was like. I talked about my own experience and that gave them confidence. It was like that old saying, 'Been there, done that, got the T-shirt!' The therapists told me that I often found out more about what the patients were thinking and feeling than the mental health staff did. I think it was because the patients had confidence in me and trusted me. They all opened up to me because they knew I understood; I'd had the same experience. It was important for me to know that I was able to give something back. But without the course and going back to college, none of that would have happened.

Other things have changed as well. My confidence has grown so much – not just since the breakdown but overall as well. I used to hate talking on the telephone. I was always self-conscious and never felt that I had the right words. But now I'll chat with anyone, I'm not shy or self-conscious. I am still at college studying ceramics. I am also hoping to take an adult teaching course so I can teach Art for Health, a creative therapy course. One of the patients at the hospital enrolled at the Wolverhampton Adult Education Service on my advice. I encouraged him and told him not to worry about being on his own on the first day. I told him that everyone would be supportive and he'd soon meet people – and he did.

When I was at school, if a teacher mentioned homework or study, I just ignored it. I couldn't see the point. Back then, I never believed in myself, and no one else seemed to believe in me either. But it really is never too late. People just don't realize that there is so much help out there, in so many different places. You just have to ask and, if you don't get an answer first time, keep asking until you do. The adult education centre has become like a family to me. Just like the best kind of family, it gives me the support and encouragement to make the most of myself and to help other people to do that for themselves too. Of course I wouldn't have done any of this if I had not been so ill. It's funny how things can work out for the better.

The Actress

Louise Jameson's acting career was hugely successful. She was Leela in Dr Who *and Rosa di Marco in* EastEnders. *But life at home was quite different from the glamorous lifestyle her fans might have imagined.*

Louise Jameson

I always knew I would be an actor. I am not sure how it happened. It's just like the facts of life – I always knew! I didn't come from a particularly theatrical family; acting was just something I was good at. When I was four I played Little Miss Muffet at primary school and adored it! I got a huge round of applause and a lot of giggling and I just loved the feedback from the audience. At one point I wanted to be a dancer. Then I wanted to be a concert pianist. In my teens, I decided I had to focus on one interest, music or acting, because they are both so time consuming. So the piano went and Shakespeare took over.

I realize now that I was dyslexic at school, but

in my day it was not really recognized. The method of teaching then was to make students learn things by heart. That suited me: I could just memorize words and sentences, and didn't really have to understand them or recognize them if they were written down.

Things really took off for me after a rather ordinary school life. I went to RADA – the Royal Academy of Dramatic Art – and then took a job with the Royal Shakespeare Company. Theatre was my great love but lots of film and television work followed – two series of *Dr Who* as well as *EastEnders*, *Bergerac*, *The Bill*, *Doctors* and others. But the big problem facing a dyslexic actor is, of course, how do you learn your lines? Dyslexics often have a problem with their short-term memory, and this can make things rather tricky. But I found one thing that made a huge difference: I got tape recordings of the scripts, and I learned my lines by listening to the tapes. But, even today, I still struggle with things like directions. I have absolutely no sense of where I am going – to me, a map is like looking at scrambled eggs on a plate and trying to sort the yolk from the white!

For two years I played the widow Rosa di Marco in *EastEnders*. Rosa always seemed to be fretting about her family, and, at times, I felt just the same. My two sons, Harry and Tom, are by far my best-ever productions. But I could see that they too were having the same difficulties that I'd had at school, and I was trying so hard to find ways to help them. What people often don't realize is that no two dyslexics are the same. It is like a fingerprint; they are all individual, and they need different solutions to suit their needs.

As Tom got close to school age he still couldn't recognize letters of the alphabet, let alone write his own name. He found it all so frustrating. When he was diagnosed (aged seven) it didn't help because we knew he had a problem, but didn't know what to do with it.

The British Dyslexia Association believes that dyslexia affects up to 10 per cent of children and that it causes problems across the spectrum – reading, writing, spelling, understanding numbers and organizing things. I spent a lot of money trying to help both boys. I employed private tutors but Tom, especially, still found it so hard. Homework time was very frustrating and became a source of frequent arguments. I tried everything: offering rewards, giving lots of encouragement, even just plain nagging, but none of it worked. He was bored and fed up, and I was tearing my hair out. I knew Tom was intelligent but I had no idea how to bring it out.

I tried to read everything I could find about dyslexia. It was clear that dyslexic people are often very intelligent. For instance, many dyslexics become architects because it's a job that allows them to express ideas in a different way from just using words. They are not confined to a simple two-dimensional way of thinking. They can get across their ideas in all sorts of ways. But the modern ways of learning and teaching just don't suit the problems that dyslexic people face.

We still hadn't solved the problem by the time Tom left school, and his memories of his school years are not very happy ones. Because he was struggling so much, he tried to find other ways of coping, like playing the class clown. It made the other kids laugh, but the teachers only saw him as naughty. He'd do anything to avoid things like reading aloud, including getting sent out of the classroom for playing up. It meant that he was punished, and one of the ways the teachers punished him was by excluding him from sport, the one thing he loved and at which he was very good.

The breakthrough came with a gift from my homeopathic doctor – *The Gift of Dyslexia*, a book by Ronald D. Davis. I read every word of that book and, for the first time, I stopped thinking of dyslexia as a handicap. I only wish I'd read it sooner. It totally changed how I saw dyslexia. I found a website, The Learning People, that specialized in treatments. On it I found details of the Davis Dyslexia Correction Programme, which has been used in America since the 1980s and in Britain since 1997. I enrolled Tom on the programme. He was 19 at the time. It was not cheap but for us it was well worth it, and I would really encourage any parent to do the same, if it seems the right thing. It's an investment in your child's future.

Part of the therapy programme is to shape words in plasticine: this helps a lot of dyslexics to understand the letters and words because they frequently find it hard to recognize letters when they are written on a page. Dyslexic people often see things from all sorts of angles – in a three-dimensional way – and that can make it hard to read and write words, because text can seem like it is moving around. This goes back to my point about architects. They don't think in a two-dimensional way; they see buildings and living spaces in many different ways. This was the key to unlocking Tom's problem. It was very, very hard work but worth it.

The intensive programme changed Tom's

life. Even after the first day, I saw positive changes in him. It was so wonderful to watch the way he responded. It was very emotional as I remembered the 15 years we'd spent trying to teach him how to write. His writing was once almost impossible to read but he can now write well. His reading has improved so much that he really enjoys it.

Being able to read and write gave Tom the skills to start on a proper career. Suddenly he had the confidence to take up something he really wanted to do, like sport. Now, at the age of 23, he's a qualified personal trainer. He passed all the exams and was able to learn the names of all the different muscles, which he would never have been able to do before. He also looks much healthier because he works out; he is not the skinny, unconfident, unhappy boy about whom I used to worry so much.

My own experience and my sons' struggles have meant that I see it as my mission to make people aware of the help that exists for dyslexic people. What made the big difference for us was The Learning People, and I would encourage anyone interested to take a look at their website. But there are lots and lots of other ways to get help as well. There are many things you can do to find something that works for you or your child. Everyone is different, and there is not just one way to help; there are many ways. And always tell yourself that dyslexia is not a handicap. It is a form of intelligence and a very valuable one at that. It can be a gift.

(www.thelearningpeople.co.uk)

The Student

Pure joy at overcoming her long-term problems shines through Pam Hopkins's words. She is an active woman in her 70s, loving every minute of her new lease of life. Here's to the next twenty years, Pam.

Pam Hopkins

When many people think about the Second World War these days, they probably think of it more like a historical film or a TV series. But for me, and people of my generation, it was real life not an adventure story. I was a child in Swansea during the war. The city was badly bombed, because the port was a target for the Nazi planes. We could hear the bombs exploding from our house. Just like in London, the local children were evacuated to the countryside, where their parents thought they would be safe. Between the ages of seven and 11, I lived in two different homes in the Welsh Valleys. One was owned by a major and another by a widow. It wasn't that bad, although I did get homesick for my family. I went to school and learnt in Welsh, but I don't remember learning very much.

When I was 11 I was sent to a convent boarding school. My grandfather was very ill, so my mother couldn't cope with looking after me as well. The nuns taught me the Christian catechism but not much else. I felt like I was really there to help with the chores and do different jobs. I used to have to fetch the coal for the fires, to sweep and dust. The school also kept chickens, and it was my special job to feed the chickens with the leftovers from meals and to collect the eggs. I loved collecting the eggs; it was so exciting – how many would there be today. Once I collected an egg that was perfect in every way apart from the fact it didn't have a shell – just a thin skin, a membrane. Picking it up was like picking up something incredibly vulnerable. I'll never forget it.

I left the convent to go to a small private school in Swansea. I was very lucky – my education was quite privileged. But life had been disrupted, and I never really mastered the basics, so I left school with no qualifications at all.

In those days you took a job where you could; there was never much thought of having a real career, especially for a woman. You knew you just had to go out and earn money. My mother arranged for me to work for the local dentist. I lived in their house and helped out with the chores. During this time, I met my husband at a local dance. He was a doctor. He had been to Oxford University and was very clever, but he never, ever tried to make me feel stupid. He was a very kind man. I learnt so many life skills from him but I still could not really read or write. He knew but never said anything, to protect my feelings.

We had three sons, and I was determined that their education would be a good one. I had such problems trying to understand the letters that the school used to send home to the parents. I would think up ways to hide the fact that I couldn't read properly. For example, I used to pretend to be too busy with something else to have time to read the letter, that way I didn't have to try to make sense of the words. But, of course I needed to know what was actually in the letter, so I would then casually call out to the boys, 'What did that letter say?', and they'd read it to me without suspecting anything. When they were little I used to hear them read, but could not really help if they got stuck on any words. As young as they were, their reading

62

was better than mine. My husband and I were so proud when one of our sons won a scholarship.

My home life kept me extremely busy for many years. I was very dedicated to my family. When the boys were older, I wanted to spread my wings a bit and so I took a job as a domestic in a local hospital. I worked there for 25 years and I loved it; I did not need to read or write for the job which was a great relief.

My husband died ten years ago and I missed him a lot. I'd often watch TV on my own at home and I kept seeing an advertisement on the BBC for something called the Learning Zone. I ignored it at first, but after three or four more times I started to get interested. I told myself that, if it came on again, I should call the number and find out more. When the advertisement came on again, I phoned the helpline. A lovely, friendly woman answered and reassured me that I was certainly not too old to learn. She arranged for me to visit my local college in Swansea. I wanted to learn to read and write. My tutor said I was not actually dyslexic but that I would be in that class at first, just to give me a good start. Everyone was really friendly, and no one was rude about my age.

I learnt quickly, and before long I could pick

up any newspaper or book and make my way through it. I have read all sorts of things and one of my favourite books is *A Tale of Two Cities* by Charles Dickens. We read it in class and I loved it. One day my lecturer told me I had done so well that my name had been put forward for an adult learning award. I was amazed that this could happen to me at my age. I got a certificate and won £50. It might seem like a small award but it really meant the world to me. I have taken so many tests since I started college that I have lost count. Each one seems like a new challenge, but it's such a thrill when I take on each challenge and just stick with it until I finish.

I may be in my seventies, but I'm a student who is young at heart. I still go to college each week. It's four miles away and I get the bus and then walk, so I get to exercise my brain and my body as well. One time, I was making a cup of tea and there was a group of women in the room. They asked me my age and were so thrilled they were not the oldest at college. They had come to learn the basics as well and I told them all the things I had learnt. They said they were all struggling with reading and writing, and I was able to tell them that they were in the best place to learn.

When people talk about things that excite them, you never, ever hear them say that one of those things is being able to read the writing on a prescription. Yet that, to me, is a cause of great excitement these days. Until I was 70 I had to get someone to read a prescription for me and then read out the information on the medicine bottle or packet. Now I can do it myself.

I would say to anyone who thinks it's too late for them – it's never too late. Just look at me! It goes to show that age can never stop you from learning. I am a living example of that. Age is just a state of mind. Experts say that the best way to keep your mind bright and alert is to learn new things. Don't ever let your age get in your way.

Helping the Community

Sometimes the best way of seeing a person's story is through someone else's eyes. Laura's and Angela's stories show that whatever hardships you face, they can be overcome with the right help and support.

Carol Taylor, Director of the Basic Skills Agency, NIACE (National Institute of Adult Continuing Education)

I felt like I had been given this giant bag of sweets when I was appointed director of a new reading and writing project in Derbyshire. Read On – Write Away! started in 1997 and was funded by a £200,000 grant from Derbyshire County Council. Our aim was to be rooted in the community, and ten years on that is still how it works. When I left in 2003 to take up a national post, it was like leaving my baby. My passion has always been to share skills with others, who can pass them on again.

We were able to change people's lives with the Derbyshire project. There are so many great examples. One was Laura: she'd been placed in care as a baby and had 16 different homes in 16 years. Not surprisingly she did not settle anywhere and could not wait to run her own life – as she said: 'The minute I was 16, I was off – I had not attended school much anyway. I played truant all the time with my friends. Some of the schools I had gone to weren't bad. It was just that I had never been anywhere long enough to settle in and learn much. My reading was OK but not great, my writing was basic and I had never taken any exams. I wasn't that good with money and ended up living in all sorts of different places. Sometimes I was on the street.'

Laura came across the Buddy Reading Project through the children's charity Barnardo's, which had offered her support when she left the care system at the age of 16. She saw an advert for the project and thought that helping five year olds each week in school, with the chance of some extra learning herself, would be a good idea. It gave her a sense of responsibility. She said, 'What I really liked was that you had to sign up properly with a contract, or not bother. It was no good doing it one week and not the next. They explained to me that I had to keep my side of the bargain as the kids would be waiting for me to turn up.'

The first morning she went to the local infant

school, Laura was really nervous. She said, 'I thought, what if I don't know what to say? What if they ask me something really difficult?' But the kids were thrilled to see her; they asked about her tattoos, and her big earrings were a great talking point. In her first session she read *The Very Hungry Caterpillar* to a five-year-old girl. 'We then talked about the book and my tattoos, and the time went really quickly,' Laura said. Her contract was for ten weeks, and she never missed any of the sessions. She said, 'I walked into that classroom twice a week and they just came running to me. They didn't know I had been in care, they didn't know I had struggled with a drug problem – they just liked me.'

At one point Laura was forced to leave the squat where she'd been living and was homeless, but, despite living on the streets at the time, she still went into the school for every session. It gave her a boost to know that she was valued and that people took her seriously. She said, 'I loved going into the staff room and just listening to all the adults talking about things. No one ever criticized me about anything, and this was the first time I thought I could do something more with my life.'

Laura extended her contract with the school

and started on some basic skills courses to improve her English and maths. She said that the confidence she gained from reading to children made her think about others and what she could offer: 'I started to become more self-confident. I was in charge and being treated as an adult.' After passing a number of exams, Laura got enough qualifications to get a paid job in the school where she had been a Reading Buddy.

Another inspiring woman who came through our programme was Angela. She lived on a very deprived council estate, where we'd placed advertisements about our family literacy group. She came along after her child started school, because she could not help him with his homework. She learnt quickly and went on to do an IT/computer course with the hope of getting a job at the end of it. But then things seemed to fall apart. Her husband left her; she dropped out of the group, and we couldn't contact her. We did finally track her down through friends, but it was sad to see that she had lost all her confidence. After a year she came back and finished her English GCSE. Then her youngest son was diagnosed with serious epilepsy. But this time she did not disappear when things got bad. She took action instead. Through his school, she set up a support group for mothers with special needs children.

Angela told us that the literacy group and passing exams had helped her regain her confidence. Her communication skills and courage had improved so much that she felt she was ready to put herself forward to lead local groups, and later she became a school governor. Angela also trained to become a community worker, and now works on the estate where she lives. She is making a real difference to people's lives. And she's telling everyone about what education has done for her – and what it can do for them.

In one small village in Derbyshire, we did some research among the women. We asked them what they thought was the best age to start reading to their children. They all said 'at about four'. Ask any expert, and they will say you cannot start too soon, because what a child learns in the first three years is so important. Through health visitors we started a Books for Babies project: when a baby turned nine months, the mother was given a gift bag with various leaflets and a book. It was very much aimed at single parents.

After the project had been running in that same Derbyshire village for a few years, we went back and asked the same question. This time everyone replied, 'before the children turn one'. It was great to see how they had changed their minds. They'd been able to see for themselves the huge benefits of reading to children from such a young age. And they realized that such a simple thing could have far-reaching effects that would help the children throughout their school years and into adulthood.

The Writer

If you are 'classed as thick', it's all too easy to write yourself off as dim and worthless. Tina is living proof that if you have the drive to see beyond that insulting label, you can amaze yourself with your breadth of achievement and excitement.

Tina Hewitt

I had so many problems trying to read books that I never imagined I'd get to the point where I would ever think of writing one. But I have started writing my own book and I want it to be part of the Quick Reads series. I want to tell my story that way, because it is the Quick Reads books that have given me the most wonderful new start and the confidence to change my life.

I was born and brought up in Hull. I love the place, but it's obviously had its problems in the recent past because of the closure of so much industry. As with other large cities, estates were built that weren't, with hindsight, the best places for people to live. There were real problems for those of us who lived there. It was a hotbed of unhappiness, really. There were a lot of people with too little money and too many problems all living on top of each other. Somehow minor things become issues, and you end up wondering how you became so petty. Mind you, balancing that, you also have a great deal of support from people around you – and that counts for a lot.

I had real learning difficulties at school, but no one picked up on them. When I had problems understanding some areas of school work or needed a bit of extra help, I was just classed as thick and the teachers gave up on me. I left with no qualifications, not even GCSEs. I got a job in a factory and then worked as a nanny before having children. My three kids are now teenagers. As they got older, I decided that I really needed to do something more than just be a mum. My friend Susan, who has five children, felt exactly the same way. We started to think of other possibilities.

With eight children between us, we felt we had a lot of experience of the education system. My own school days were far behind me, but I hadn't forgotten the problems I had experienced there. I remembered how unhappy I'd been, without anyone to take the time really to understand why I wasn't learning very much. I felt it would be worthwhile to train as a teaching assistant. Susan and I went along to the Women's Centre in Hull, where they ran a training course. We enrolled and made a good start with our studies, but we felt like we'd hit a brick wall when it came to maths and English. We both struggled so much that we knew we needed to sort that out, or face having to give up the course. We were determined to stick with it and not just give up when the going got tough. Instead, we enrolled on a basic maths and English course at our local college.

One day in our English class, the tutor came in with a large pile of books in the Quick Reads series. We could all choose one to take home to read. Quick Reads are designed for people who like reading, but who also find reading boring or difficult, so they were ideal for me. From the first page, I knew I had at last found a book that I could read easily and understand. I realized I could actually finish a book, rather than be put off by the time I had got to the end of the first page, which is what usually happened. I'd lost count of the number of books I'd wanted to read in the past. I'd just get so fed up with struggling with words I couldn't understand, that I'd give up and feel like throwing the book at the nearest wall!

The first Quick Reads I took home was Tom Holt's *Someone Like Me*. It was brilliant and enjoyable to read. It was an exciting science-fiction fantasy story set far into the future. It describes how a terrible event has taken place and humans are being hunted by a group called Them. I couldn't put it down. On the back of the book, the description read, 'In a world torn apart by hatred and fear, only the strong survive.' I thought that could apply to lots of things – not just this book. When your own private world is full of fear and worries, you do have to be strong to survive. It can be scary, taking on things that you might find hard, but I'd done it; it had taken a lot of strength and I had survived.

There are lots of Quick Reads books, and it made me want to read every single one. The next one I chose was *Chickenfeed* by Minette Walters. It was a crime thriller based on a real-life story about what was called 'the chicken farm murder' in East Sussex back in 1924. This book won the Quick Reads Learners' Favourite Award in 2006. It told the story of a man accused of killing his girlfriend, and you really got to know the two main characters, Norman and Elsie. I knew Minette had written lots of crime books but I'd never read any of them.

This was such a great way of realizing that I could pick up one of the longer ones and be able to read it.

Next on my list was a book by John Bird, the man who started the *Big Issue*, the magazine sold by people who live on the streets. That book was called *How to Change Your Life in 7 Steps*. It was such an inspiring read by a man who'd had hard times himself, yet had achieved so much. He gives seven simple rules to follow to achieve your goals – maybe getting a new job, or giving up smoking or drinking, or going back to college. He explains how you can take what life has given you, no matter how bad, and turn it into something of which you'll be proud. As he says, there's no point in just wishing things were different and thinking that you are a victim all the time, blaming every-thing and everybody. You have to think for yourself, if you want to improve your life. You have to get out and do it yourself. I learnt a lot of good ideas from that book.

Out of the blue, our tutor invited us down to London to meet some of the Quick Reads authors. We couldn't believe it. It was such a thrill actually to meet the people who had written the books that had come to mean a lot to us. We met Minette Walters: she was lovely, and we talked about her book. We also bumped into John Bird. That was in 2006, and it was then that we knew we could do more with these books at home. By the time we got home, we were all so excited about ways to use these books and we wanted to tell other people about them. We decided that one good way to do this was to start a reading group in our local area. The idea just took off. We put up adverts around our estate. We told everybody what we were doing and even went to the local library. They were so kind. They lent us 81 Quick Reads to start us off. The reading group was ready to be launched.

That first Monday afternoon we had no idea who would come or how many people would turn up – if anyone at all. In the end, we had 12 women who were doing different courses and thought a reading group would help them. Once we were set up, it was a very easy group to run. We handed out books with a review sheet for people to fill in at home. We also made a big poster of a tree, so people could stick on what they thought of a particular Quick Reads. The group is very established now. We always start each meeting with talking about which books we are all reading. We often disagree and someone will say, 'I really couldn't get into that book.' But then someone else will say, 'But it's my favourite!', and persuade that person to give it another try. It's a very friendly atmosphere and very positive. No one is scared to say what they think, and it's good to have different opinions. It makes you think in ways that you might not have thought before. We have a good laugh; after talking about the books, we make a cup of tea and catch up on gossip. I suppose we could write a newspaper for the estate given the amount we know!

When we went back to London for the 2007 launch of Quick Reads, we showed everyone the cards we'd made up for our reading group. All the authors thought it was great and it's still going really well. But the best part of it is that it has led to lots of really positive things for women in the group. Susan and I have started up an after-school club for kids on our estate funded by a local organization, DOC (Develop Our Community) Hull. We have called our project the Back Street Kids. If we get enough funding, we should like to run something all day for kids on the estate.

It's become so important to us that our children don't give up on education. My oldest son is dyslexic; for the last two years of school I tutored him at home, and he is now at college doing a diploma in sport. I would never have had the confidence to do this before. I think, for women, the first step of going back to education can be really hard. You have to pluck up your courage, but once you've done it there is so much help.

It is very easy for women, once they have had kids, to think it is just too late to get an education, if they haven't done well first time around. If you look at my friends and me, you'll see that is just not the case. I have more confidence now than I could ever have imagined. I've got a lot of ambition and a lot of goals. I am determined to finish writing my own Quick Reads. And I shall.

The Brickie

Welcome to the dazzling story of Dawn, an amazing mother of seven who was inspired by her own father and proved herself by inheriting his proud title, Brickie.

Dawn Stokes

It's funny how life turns out. I spent much of my childhood wanting to be a boy, so I could go and work with my dad in the building trade. I sort of wanted to be my brother, so I could be part of the gang. I had always loved watching my dad making things: he was really handy and a talented bricklayer; he could do anything. I used to get quite offended when it was my brother with whom he worked and not me, but as a girl at that time I didn't really question it. But when my dad died a few years ago, it was to me he left his tools, not my brother.

I didn't get on well at school, and I really regret it. I don't think I was that academic, but it was my attitude that was the real problem. I was a teenage girl keen to grow up and earn money. So I left as soon as I could and found a job in a factory. I just wanted to have a good time and at last I had the money to do it.

But after a few years I did have these nagging doubts. Why hadn't I made more of my school life; why hadn't I got more exams? By this time I had settled down and started having a family. I had my first baby at 19 – she is now grown up – and I have a little one who has just started school. Altogether I have seven kids, so I was pretty busy for a few years. I never regret having had the kids and being around to bring them up.

Then suddenly my life changed: my marriage went wrong and my dad died. I suppose I came to a sort of crisis point. He'd left me his tools, and yet he wasn't there to show me how to use them. That nagging feeling about not doing well at school got worse that summer, and, when all the kids went back to school in September, I marched into our local college to see if there was anything I could do for myself.

I knew that what I really wanted to do was a bricklaying course, but the college said they didn't run one. I suppose I was also aware that I was not a typical student either. I kept getting told that I could do hairdressing or something they thought was more suitable for women!

I also went down to the Job Centre and asked the same thing. I met a really nice man called Gordon who took a real interest and found me a place on a taster course for civil engineering. He knew I wanted to work and train in the construction industry so this was a good start. I was told it was only for a few weeks, but I ended up staying on the course until Christmas. It was really good. I was the only woman, and the course gave me an idea of what it would be like working in that industry. Perhaps because I was older I wasn't so bothered, although I remember being really nervous on the first day. But the men were great, really helpful and friendly.

Then I went to two different colleges to ask about bricklaying courses. One told me I did not live close enough to the college, but I am quite persistent and they did let me on the course. At the same time I also discovered I had been accepted on a course at South Birmingham College, so I decided to do both as they were each only part time. But, of course, put together it was like working full time. It was a bit complicated juggling home and courses, but I managed it because I was determined to make it work.

I've now got qualifications in bricklaying and

plastering. The courses have all been very hands-on, with homework as well. I think this has suited me, as I am a practical person. Right from the start I was determined not to look an idiot in front of the men. Since doing the courses my confidence and self-esteem have gone sky-high. I got quite low during my divorce and after losing my dad. Studying has really helped improve the quality of my life and helped me cope. It just got better and better the more courses I did.

I am now shadowing a teacher with a view to getting a teaching qualification. I have also been offered a job at Sandwell College. The problem with the building industry is that it does not go well with running a family, as you can be off in a van all over the country. For the moment, teaching others like me is what I want to do. But, ultimately, I might consider setting up my own business.

My kids think it's great. My youngest is always messing about building things in our garden; she's already had a go at bricklaying. At school her whole class went to the building site, and she took my hard hat. I don't care whether my sons are ballerinas or if my girls are bricklayers. I just want them to find the right job for them, whatever that is. I would say to anyone out there with no qualifications, go to your local college and find out what they offer. It's only the first step that is difficult.

Quick Reads

Books in the Quick Reads series

www.quickreads.org.uk

Quick Reads

Pick up a book today

Quick Reads are bite-sized books by bestselling writers and well-known personalities for people who want a short, fast-paced read. They are designed to be read and enjoyed by avid readers and by people who never had or who have lost the reading habit.

Quick Reads are published alongside and in partnership with BBC RaW.

We would like to thank all our partners in the Quick Reads project for their help and support:

The Department for Innovation, Universities and Skills
NIACE
unionlearn
National Book Tokens
The Vital Link
The Reading Agency
National Literacy Trust
Welsh Books Council
Basic Skills Cymru, Welsh Assembly Government
Wales Accent Press
Lifelong Learning Scotland
DELNI
NALA

Quick Reads would also like to thank the Department for Innovation, Universities and Skills; Arts Council England and World Book Day for their sponsorship and NIACE for their outreach work.

Quick Reads is a World Book Day initiative.
www.quickreads.org.uk   www.worldbookday.com

Quick Reads

Happy Families

Adele Parks

Penguin

Lisa is forty-two, divorced and a mum of three. For the past year, she has been going out with Mark, who is five years younger than her. Lisa really likes him but she worries that one day he will leave – just like her ex-husband did. On top of everything else, Lisa feels really tired and moody, and has put on weight. She thinks it's the menopause but could there be another reason for how she's feeling?

Lisa's life is about to change in a big way but does she want Mark by her side? Does he even want to be there? With the help of her family and friends, Lisa starts to believe that a second chance of love and happiness might just be possible . . .

Quick Reads

The 10 Keys to Success
John Bird

Vermillion

Are you struggling to achieve what you want?

John Bird, founder of *The Big Issue*, will show you just how simple success can be.

John gives simple practical tips and advice, such as 'Stop looking for approval from others' and 'Start with small steps'. In this way he shows us that we can all achieve whatever we want. We just need to go after it.

Quick Reads

East End Tales
Gilda O'Neill

Penguin

Gilda O'Neill was born in London's East End. Her nan had a pie and mash shop and her grandfather was a tug-boat skipper. You might think Gilda's childhood was filled with knees-ups in pubs and famous criminals – but that is just half the story. In *East End Tales*, Gilda tells what the true East End was like – not the place of myth and legend. Tales of hardship and upheaval rub shoulders with stories of kindness, pride, courage and humour.

Quick Reads

Life's New Hurdles
Colin Jackson

Accent Press

Colin Jackson is one of the greatest athletes that Britain has ever produced. He was in the world top ten for 16 years, and was world number 1 for two of them. He set seven European and Commonwealth and nine UK records and he still holds the world record for indoor hurdling.

In 2003, Colin retired from athletics in front of an adoring home crowd. Then real life began. In *Life's New Hurdles* Colin describes the shock of adjusting to sudden change. From athletics commentating to sports presenting and *Strictly Come Dancing*, Colin describes the challenges and joys of starting a whole new life.

Quick Reads

Humble Pie
Gordon Ramsay

HarperCollins

Everyone thinks they know the real Gordon Ramsay: rude, loud, driven, stubborn. But this is his real story . . .

Gordon tells the extraordinary story of how he became the world's most famous chef: his difficult childhood, his failed first career as a footballer, his TV personality – all the things that have made him the media star that he is today.

Other resources

Free courses are available for anyone who wants to develop their skills. You can attend the courses in your local area. If you'd like to find out more, phone 0800 66 0800.

A list of books for new readers can be found on www.firstchoicebooks.org.uk or at your local library.

Publishers Barrington Stoke (www.barringtonstoke.co.uk), New Island (www.newisland.ie) and Sandstone Press (www.sandstonepress.com) also provide books for new readers.

The BBC runs a reading and writing campaign. See www.bbc.co.uk/raw.

2008 is a National Year of Reading. To find out more, search online, see www.dius.gov.uk or visit your local library.

www.quickreads.org.uk　　　www.worldbookday.com